RANJOT SINGH CHAHAL

# Perfectly Act Like Success

*A Step-by-Step Guide to Achieving Success*

Rana Books

*First published by Rana Books ( UK, India )  2023*

*Copyright © 2023 by Ranjot Singh Chahal*

*All rights reserved. No part of this publication may be reproduced, stored or transmitted in any form or by any means, electronic, mechanical, photocopying, recording, scanning, or otherwise without written permission from the publisher. It is illegal to copy this book, post it to a website, or distribute it by any other means without permission.*

*First edition*

*ISBN: 978-93-91927-98-1*

# Contents

1. Introduction — 1
2. Understanding Success — 4
3. Self-Reflection and Awareness — 7
4. Setting Goals for Success — 11
5. Building a Winning Mindset — 16
6. Developing Essential Skills for Success — 20
7. Building Relationships for Success — 24
8. Taking Action and Persisting Towards Success — 30
9. Maintaining Work-Life Balance — 34
10. Celebrating Success and Embracing Growth — 38
11. 100 Tips for Success — 42

# 1

# Introduction

Welcome to a transformative journey towards personal and professional success. In "Perfectly Act Like Success: A Step-by-Step Guide to Achieving Success," we embark on a voyage of self-discovery, goal setting, and skill development. Success isn't a mystery; it's a series of intentional actions and mindsets. In this book, we'll explore the fundamental principles that empower you to define and achieve your version of success. Whether you seek career advancement, personal growth, or simply a more fulfilling life, the insights and strategies within these pages will be your compass. So, let's begin this exciting journey to unlock your full potential and become the success you aspire to be.

1.1 Welcome to the World of Success:

Welcome to the world of success! This is a place where individuals strive to achieve their goals fulfill their potential and lead a fulfilling and prosperous life. Success can have different meanings for different people as it encompasses various aspects of life such as personal growth professional achievements financial stability and overall well-being.

To embark on the journey of success it is essential to have a clear vision of what success means to you. It could be obtaining a specific career milestone starting a successful business maintaining healthy relationships or simply finding happiness and contentment in life. Identifying your unique definition of success will guide your actions and decisions.

Success is not a destination but rather a continuous process. It requires dedication hard work perseverance and a willingness to step out of your comfort zone. It involves setting realistic goals creating a plan and taking consistent action towards achieving those goals. Along the way there may be obstacles and challenges but these should be viewed as opportunities for growth and learning.

1.2 Setting the Stage for Personal and Professional Growth:

Setting the stage for personal and professional growth is crucial for achieving success. Personal growth involves enhancing your knowledge skills and mindset while professional growth focuses on advancing your career and achieving success in your chosen field. These two aspects are interconnected and can amplify each other.

Personal growth includes continuous learning self-reflection and self-improvement. It involves acquiring new skills expanding your knowledge base and developing a growth mindset.

For example if you aspire to become a successful entrepreneur you might invest time in learning about business strategies networking financial management or leadership skills.

Professional growth entails setting career goals seeking opportunities for advancement and developing a strong professional network. It involves staying up to date with industry trends embracing new technologies and expanding your professional expertise. For instance if you want to excel in your career as a software engineer you might focus on improving your coding skills staying updated with the latest programming languages or pursuing certifications in relevant areas.

Both personal and professional growth require setting clear goals and developing actionable plans to achieve them. It is also essential to cultivate a growth mindset which involves embracing challenges seeking feedback and being open to learning from both successes and failures.

By actively focusing on personal and professional growth you lay the foundation for long-term success. Continuous improvement and adaptability become ingrained in your mindset allowing you to navigate the ever-evolving landscape of personal and professional life.

In summary success is a journey that requires a clear vision hard work and consistent effort. By setting the stage for personal and professional growth you create the conditions necessary for success to flourish. Embrace the opportunities for growth learn from your experiences and keep pushing yourself to reach new heights. Success awaits you!

# 2

# Understanding Success

Success is a multifaceted jewel, its facets reflecting diverse dreams and aspirations. In this chapter, we embark on a quest to unravel the intricate tapestry of success. We'll challenge conventional notions and ask the fundamental question: What does success truly mean to you? As we delve into the psychology of success, we discover the remarkable power of mindset and beliefs in shaping our journeys. Through the inspiring stories of those who defied odds, we'll see how success often emerges from the fertile ground of a growth mindset. This chapter serves as a compass, guiding you to identify your unique definition of success, a pivotal step on the path to personal and professional achievement. Get ready to navigate the terrain of success with clarity and purpose, as we set the stage for your transformative journey.

2.1 Defining Success: What Does it Really Mean?

Defining success is a highly subjective matter because it means different things to different people. Society often portrays success in terms of wealth power and status. However true success goes beyond these external markers and is deeply personal. It involves aligning your goals values and passions with your actions and achievements.

To define success for yourself it's essential to reflect on your desires dreams and aspirations. Consider what truly matters to you in life and what you want to achieve. Success can mean reaching specific career milestones cultivating strong relationships achieving personal growth making a positive impact on others or finding inner peace and happiness. Remember that your definition of success should be authentic to you and not solely influenced by societal expectations.

2.2 The Psychology of Success: Mindset and Beliefs

The psychology of success revolves around the beliefs and mindset that shape our thoughts actions and outcomes. Your beliefs about success can either propel you forward or hold you back. Developing a growth mindset which embraces challenges learns from failures and seeks self-improvement is crucial for cultivating success.

It's important to challenge limiting beliefs that may hinder your progress. Common examples include the belief that success is reserved for a select few or that failure equates to personal inadequacy. By shifting your perspective and seeing failure as a stepping stone to growth you can overcome obstacles and achieve success.

Positive self-talk and visualization techniques can also help rewire your subconscious mind to align with your pursuit of success. By affirming positive beliefs and imagining yourself achieving your goals you can enhance your motivation confidence and overall success.

### 2.3 Identifying Your Unique Definition of Success

To identify your unique definition of success it's crucial to understand your values passions and life purpose. Ask yourself introspective questions such as:

- What do I value most in life? Is it financial security personal relationships or making a difference in the world?
- What activities or pursuits bring me joy and fulfillment?
- What impact do I want to have on others and the world around me?
- What are my long-term goals and aspirations?
- How do I want to feel when I consider myself successful?

Reflecting on these questions allows you to align your definition of success with your authentic self. Remember that success is a journey and your definition may evolve over time as you grow and change. Embrace the process of self-discovery and continually reassess your goals and values to ensure they align with your evolving definition of success.

In conclusion defining success is a deeply personal and subjective process. It involves understanding your unique values passions and aspirations. Cultivating a growth mindset and challenging limiting beliefs is crucial for achieving success. Remember that success is not solely defined by societal standards but by how well your actions achievements and sense of fulfillment align with your authentic self.

# 3

# Self-Reflection and Awareness

Self-reflection and awareness are the mirrors through which we begin to truly see ourselves. They are the quiet moments of introspection that hold the power to reshape our lives. In this chapter, we'll embark on a journey of self-discovery, exploring the art of looking inward to understand our values, beliefs, and motivations. By embracing self-awareness, we gain the key to unlock our potential, identify our strengths and weaknesses, and pave the way for personal and professional growth. Through practical exercises and deep reflection, we'll illuminate the path to a more profound understanding of ourselves, setting the stage for transformative change and a richer, more purposeful life.

3.1 The Power of Self-Reflection:

Self-reflection is the process of introspection and examining one's thoughts feelings and actions. It involves taking a step back from the external distractions and focusing inwardly to gain a deeper understanding of oneself. Self-reflection allows individuals to gain insights into their behaviors motivations and beliefs leading to personal growth and development.

Example of self-reflection:

Let's say you have recently ended a long-term relationship and are feeling a mix of emotions. Through self-reflection you may ask yourself questions such as: What were my contributions to the relationship? What patterns or behaviors did I notice? How did I handle conflicts? By reflecting on these questions and examining your actions you may gain valuable insights into your relationship dynamics and identify areas for improvement or personal growth.

3.2 Uncovering and Acknowledging Your Strengths and Weaknesses:

Self-awareness involves recognizing and understanding our strengths and weaknesses. It is essential to identify and acknowledge these aspects of ourselves to effectively navigate our personal and professional lives.

Examples of uncovering and acknowledging strengths and weaknesses:

Let's consider a scenario where you are applying for a new job. Through self-awareness you can identify your strengths such as strong communication skills adaptability or problem-solving abilities. By acknowledging these strengths you can highlight them during the job interview and showcase how they align with the position's requirements.

On the other hand self-awareness also helps in recognizing weaknesses. For instance if you struggle with time management acknowledging this weakness allows you to seek solutions and develop strategies to improve your efficiency and productivity in the workplace.

3.3 Building Self-Awareness for Personal Growth:

Self-awareness lays the foundation for personal growth. By understanding ourselves better we can make conscious choices adopt healthier habits and work towards becoming the best version of ourselves.

Examples of building self-awareness for personal growth:

Let's say you want to improve your emotional intelligence. You can start by reflecting on your emotional triggers understanding how you typically express and manage your emotions and identifying any patterns or areas where you could enhance your emotional intelligence. With this awareness you can then engage in activities like journaling seeking feedback from others or practicing mindfulness to develop your emotional intelligence skills.

Similarly self-awareness can be applied to personal development in various areas such as improving communication managing stress or enhancing decision-making abilities. By building self-awareness in these areas individuals can identify and address their limitations set realistic goals and take consistent steps towards personal growth.

In conclusion self-reflection uncovering strengths and weaknesses and building self-awareness are powerful tools for personal growth. These practices allow individuals to gain insights make informed decisions and take deliberate actions to continually improve themselves. By developing self-awareness individuals can enhance various aspects of their lives and achieve their full potential.

# 4

# Setting Goals for Success

Goals are the compass points that guide us toward our desired destinations, and success, in its many forms, is often born from the seeds of well-defined objectives. In this chapter, we embark on a journey of intentional goal-setting, where dreams become tangible targets. We'll unveil the significance of setting clear and meaningful goals, exploring the SMART criteria that transform aspirations into actionable plans. By developing a strategic action plan, we'll equip you with the tools to traverse the path to success. This chapter serves as the blueprint for your future achievements, as we illuminate the process of turning your aspirations into concrete realities, setting the stage for your personal and professional growth.

4.1 The Importance of Setting Clear and Meaningful Goals:

Setting clear and meaningful goals is essential for personal and professional growth. When you have a clear goal in mind it provides you with a sense of direction purpose and motivation. Without clear goals you may find yourself wandering aimlessly and feeling unfulfilled.

Clear goals help you prioritize your tasks and focus your efforts in a specific direction. They provide a framework for decision-making and allow you to allocate your time and resources effectively. When you have a clear goal it becomes easier to identify opportunities and obstacles along the way enabling you to make strategic choices that align with your objectives.

Moreover setting meaningful goals ensures that you are working towards something that truly matters to you. Meaningful goals reflect your values passions and aspirations. They give you a sense of fulfillment and satisfaction when achieved enhancing your overall well-being and happiness. Meaningful goals provide a sense of purpose helping you stay motivated and resilient during challenging times.

Example: Let's consider a personal example. Say your goal is to lead a healthier lifestyle. A clear and meaningful goal in this context could be to exercise for at least 30 minutes every day eat a balanced diet and reduce stress levels. By setting this goal you have a clear direction and purpose in mind leading you towards improved physical and mental well-being.

4.2 SMART Goal Setting: Making Goals Specific Measurable Achievable Relevant and Time-Bound:

When setting goals it is helpful to use the SMART framework which ensures that your goals are well-defined and actionable. SMART stands for Specific Measurable Achievable Relevant and Time-Bound.

- Specific: Your goals should be specific and focused clearly stating what you want to achieve. Vague goals like "get in shape" are less effective than specific goals like "lose 10 pounds in three months by exercising three times a week and following a healthy diet."

- Measurable: Set goals that are measurable allowing you to track your progress and determine when you have achieved them. Measurable goals provide tangible evidence of your success or indicate areas where you need to adjust your efforts. For example instead of saying "read more books set a goal to "read 20 books by the end of the year."

- Achievable: Make sure your goals are realistic and attainable. Setting overly ambitious or unattainable goals can lead to frustration and discouragement. It is essential to consider your resources abilities and constraints when setting goals. An achievable goal could be "increase sales by 10% in the next quarter."

- Relevant: Ensure that your goals are relevant and aligned with your overall objectives and values. Your goals should be in harmony with your long-term vision and provide value and meaning to your life. For example if you are passionate about environmental conservation a relevant goal could be "reduce personal carbon footprint by 30% in the next year."

- Time-Bound: Set a specific timeline for achieving your goals. Deadlines add a sense of urgency and prevent procrastination. A time-bound goal could be "complete a certification program within six months."

Example: Using the SMART framework let's take the goal of writing a book. A SMART goal would be "Write a 50000-word novel in six months by dedicating two hours every day to writing outlining the chapters and seeking feedback from a writing group." This goal is specific measurable achievable relevant and time-bound.

4.3 Developing a Strategic Action Plan to Reach Your Goals:

Once you have set clear and SMART goals it is essential to create a strategic action plan to reach them. A strategic action plan outlines the steps and resources needed to accomplish your goals effectively. It helps you stay organized motivated and focused.

Here are some steps to develop a strategic action plan:

1. Break down your goals into smaller manageable tasks: Divide your goals into actionable steps that are easy to implement. This breakdown helps prevent overwhelm and provides a clear roadmap to follow.

2. Prioritize the tasks: Determine the order in which you need to tackle the tasks considering dependencies and deadlines. Prioritization ensures that you allocate your time and effort effectively.

3. Set deadlines: Assign specific deadlines to each task to create a sense of urgency and accountability. Deadlines help maintain momentum and prevent procrastination.

4. Identify necessary resources: Determine the resources you need to accomplish each task successfully. This could include time finances knowledge skills or support from others.

5. Monitor progress: Regularly track your progress to ensure you are on track. Make adjustments as needed and celebrate milestones along the way to maintain motivation.

6. Stay flexible and adaptable: Be open to adjusting your plan if circumstances change. Flexibility allows you to adapt to unforeseen challenges and seize new opportunities.

Example: Suppose your goal is to start your own business. Your strategic action plan could include tasks such as market research developing a business plan securing financing registering your business building a website and marketing your products or services. Breaking down these tasks into smaller steps and setting deadlines will help you progress towards your goal systematically.

In conclusion setting clear and meaningful goals using the SMART framework and developing a strategic action plan are vital for achieving personal and professional success. These approaches provide clarity direction and motivation helping you stay focused and accountable throughout your journey.

# 5

# Building a Winning Mindset

The mind is both our greatest ally and fiercest adversary on the road to success. In this chapter, we embark on a transformative journey into the realm of mindset, where the seeds of triumph are sown. We will explore the profound impact of beliefs, attitudes, and mental fortitude in shaping our destinies. Drawing inspiration from those who turned setbacks into stepping stones, we'll uncover the power of a positive mindset. This chapter is your gateway to overcoming limiting beliefs and embracing the fertile ground of possibilities through visualization and affirmations. It's about cultivating a growth mindset, where failures and challenges are the raw materials of triumph. As we delve into these concepts, we set the stage for you to nurture a winning mindset that will drive your personal and professional success.

5.1 Overcoming Limiting Beliefs and Cultivating a Positive Mindset:

Limiting beliefs are the negative thoughts or beliefs that hold us back from reaching our full potential. These beliefs can stem from past experiences societal conditioning or self-doubt. Overcoming limiting beliefs involves challenging and reframing them to create a more positive and empowering mindset.

For example let's say someone has a limiting belief that they are not good enough to pursue their dream career. This belief might stem from past failures or negative feedback they received. To overcome this belief they can start by questioning its validity. They can challenge themselves with questions like "What evidence do I have to support this belief? Are there successful people in my desired field who started from a similar position? What skills and qualities do I possess that make me capable of succeeding?"

By questioning the belief and finding evidence to refute it they can start cultivating a more positive mindset. They can then replace negative self-talk with positive affirmations such as "I am capable of achieving my goals or "I have the skills and determination to succeed."

5.2 The Power of Visualization and Affirmations:

Visualization and affirmations are powerful tools for reprogramming the mind and manifesting desired outcomes. Visualization involves creating detailed mental images of the desired outcome while affirmations are positive statements that reinforce empowering beliefs.

For instance if someone wants to overcome their fear of public speaking they can visualize themselves confidently delivering a speech in front of a supportive audience. They imagine the applause and positive feedback they receive. This visualization helps train the brain to associate positive emotions with public speaking gradually reducing the fear response.

Additionally repeating affirmations like "I am a confident and eloquent speaker" or "I enjoy sharing my ideas with others" can help rewire the subconscious mind and reinforce positive beliefs about public speaking. These affirmations can be repeated daily particularly in moments of self-doubt or anxiety.

5.3 Embracing a Growth Mindset: Learning from Failure and Challenges:

A growth mindset is the belief that abilities and intelligence can be developed through dedication hard work and continuous learning. Embracing a growth mindset means seeing failures and challenges as opportunities for growth and improvement rather than setbacks.

For example if someone encounters a setback in their career such as not getting a promotion they can choose to view it as a learning experience. They can identify the areas they need to improve seek feedback from colleagues or mentors and develop a plan to enhance their skills. This mindset shift allows them to approach future challenges with resilience and curiosity.

Embracing a growth mindset also involves reframing negative self-talk and internal beliefs about intelligence and abilities. Instead of saying "I'm not smart enough they can say "I may not know it yet but I can learn." By focusing on growth individuals become more open to new possibilities and are more likely to seize opportunities for self-improvement.

Overall the process of overcoming limiting beliefs cultivating a positive mindset using visualization and affirmations and embracing a growth mindset requires self-awareness introspection and consistent practice. These approaches can help individuals unlock their full potential and achieve their goals.

# 6

# Developing Essential Skills for Success

Success is a multifaceted gem, and the skills you wield are the facets that make it shine. In this chapter, we embark on a journey to polish and refine the essential skills that pave the path to triumph. We'll delve into the art of effective communication, where verbal and non-verbal expressions become your tools for influence and connection. Time management and productivity will be dissected to empower you in navigating life's demands. The realm of problem-solving and decision-making will be unveiled as your arsenal for conquering challenges. This chapter serves as your skills workshop, providing you with the knowledge and techniques to hone these critical abilities. As we explore these essential skills for success, we set the stage for your personal and professional growth, equipping you to thrive in the complex landscape of achievement.

6.1 Communication Skills: Effective Verbal and Non-Verbal Communication

Effective communication skills are crucial for success in any professional setting. They involve both verbal and non-verbal communication techniques. Verbal communication refers to the use of spoken words to convey information while non-verbal communication refers to the use of body language gestures and facial expressions to communicate messages.

Example 1: Verbal Communication

Imagine you are attending a team meeting where you need to present a progress report. You utilize effective verbal communication skills by speaking clearly using appropriate language and organizing your thoughts in a structured manner. This helps convey your message clearly and engage your audience.

Example 2: Non-Verbal Communication

During a job interview you demonstrate strong non-verbal communication skills. You maintain good eye contact with the interviewer nod your head to indicate understanding and use open body posture to show engagement. These non-verbal cues help create a positive impression and convey your interest in the position.

6.2 Time Management and Productivity

Time management skills are essential for maximizing productivity and achieving goals efficiently. They involve setting priorities planning tasks and effectively allocating time to diffcrent activities.

Example 1: Prioritizing Tasks

You are given a project with multiple deadlines and tasks. By utilizing time management skills you prioritize the most important and urgent tasks first. This allows you to focus your energy and efforts on completing them efficiently ensuring timely delivery.

Example 2: Planning and Scheduling

To effectively manage your time you create a detailed schedule that outlines specific time slots for different activities. This includes allocating time for important tasks breaks and personal activities. By sticking to this schedule you enhance your productivity by minimizing distractions and maintaining focus.

6.3 Problem-Solving and Decision-Making Skills

Problem-solving and decision-making skills are crucial in the workplace as they enable individuals to effectively address challenges and make informed choices when faced with various situations.

Example 1: Problem-Solving

Suppose you encounter a technical issue with a computer system at work. By utilizing problem-solving skills you analyze the situation identify the root cause of the problem and explore possible solutions. Through logical reasoning and critical thinking you successfully troubleshoot the issue and resolve it.

Example 2: Decision-Making

You are part of a team that needs to choose a new marketing strategy for a product launch. Utilizing decision-making skills you gather relevant information evaluate different options and weigh the pros and cons of each. By making an informed decision you contribute to the success of the team and the organization.

Overall these skills are essential in professional settings as they enable individuals to effectively communicate manage their time and solve problems. Developing and honing these skills can contribute to career success and personal growth.

# 7

# Building Relationships for Success

Success is not a solitary journey but a collaborative dance, and relationships are the music that fuels it. In this chapter, we embark on a voyage into the intricate world of building connections that propel you forward. We'll explore the profound significance of networking and the power of cultivating a supportive circle of individuals who share your aspirations. Effective interpersonal skills will be your compass as we navigate the delicate terrain of human interaction. The art of nurturing positive relationships, both personally and professionally, will become your secret weapon in the pursuit of success. This chapter serves as your guide to forging bonds that endure, providing you with the tools and insights to create a supportive ecosystem that fosters personal and professional growth. As we delve into the dynamics of building relationships for success, we set the stage for a journey where collaboration and connection are the keys to your triumph.

7.1 The Importance of Networking and Building a Supportive Circle:

Networking and building a supportive circle are vital aspects of personal and professional growth. It involves connecting with individuals who share similar interests goals or experiences to create mutually beneficial relationships. Here are a few reasons why networking and building a supportive circle are important:

1. Access to Opportunities: By networking you can expand your professional contacts and gain access to various opportunities. This could include job openings collaborations mentorships or partnerships. Building a supportive circle allows you to tap into these opportunities and leverage the collective knowledge and resources of your network.

Example: Imagine you are a freelance graphic designer and are part of a supportive circle of fellow designers. One of your network contacts refers you to a high-profile client looking for design services. This connection could lead to a significant project and boost your career.

2. Learning and Skill Development: Networking enables you to learn from and exchange knowledge with others who possess different expertise and perspectives. By building a supportive circle you can engage in meaningful discussions attend workshops or seminars and gain insights that contribute to personal and professional growth.

Example: If you are an aspiring entrepreneur being part of a startup community can provide valuable guidance mentorship and learning opportunities. Through networking events you can connect with experienced entrepreneurs who can share their success stories challenges and provide advice for navigating the business landscape.

3. Emotional Support and Collaboration: Building a supportive circle allows you to create connections with like-minded individuals who understand your experiences challenges and aspirations. These relationships can provide emotional support during difficult times and foster collaboration to achieve common goals.

Example: Let's say you are a writer and you join a writers' group where you can share your work and receive constructive feedback. These group members become your supportive circle offering encouragement critique and sharing their experiences in navigating the writing industry. This community helps you improve your writing skills and motivates you to persevere.

7.2 Developing Effective Interpersonal Skills:

Interpersonal skills are the abilities to interact and communicate effectively with others. Developing strong interpersonal skills is crucial for establishing positive relationships resolving conflicts and succeeding in personal and professional settings. Here's why developing effective interpersonal skills is important:

1. Building Rapport: Good interpersonal skills allow you to build rapport and establish connections with others. It involves active listening empathy and effective communication. Building rapport fosters trust respect and collaboration in personal and professional relationships.

Example: In a workplace an employee with strong interpersonal skills can connect with colleagues understand their perspectives and communicate ideas clearly. This individual builds stronger working relationships and contributes to a positive and productive team environment.

2. Conflict Resolution: Effective interpersonal skills help in resolving conflicts and managing difficult situations. By understanding others' viewpoints practicing empathy and communicating assertively you can navigate conflicts and find mutually acceptable solutions.

Example: Imagine a situation where two team members have a difference of opinion on a project. Someone with strong interpersonal skills would actively listen to both parties understand their concerns and facilitate a constructive dialogue. Through effective communication and conflict resolution skills they help the team find a compromise.

3. Collaboration and Teamwork: Developing interpersonal skills enables you to work collaboratively with others leveraging their strengths to achieve common goals. It involves effective communication active participation and understanding team dynamics.

Example: In a group project effective interpersonal skills allow team members to communicate their ideas listen to others delegate tasks and work together cohesively. By fostering collaboration interpersonal skills contribute to the project's success.

7.3 Nurturing Positive Relationships in Personal and Professional Life:

Positive relationships are key to personal and professional happiness and success. Nurturing these relationships involves investing time and effort to maintain and strengthen connections. Here's why nurturing positive relationships is important:

1. Social Support: Positive relationships provide emotional support especially during challenging times. Having a support system of close friends family or colleagues can help reduce stress provide different perspectives and offer encouragement.

Example: If you are going through a difficult period in your personal life having positive relationships enables you to reach out to friends who can lend a listening ear offer advice or simply provide a sense of comfort and understanding.

2. Collaborative Opportunities: Nurturing positive relationships can lead to collaborative opportunities in both personal and professional realms. By maintaining strong connections you can leverage each other's strengths knowledge and resources to achieve common goals.

Example: Let's say you are a marketing professional looking to expand your business network. By nurturing positive relationships with other professionals in related fields you may receive referrals joint venture opportunities or access to new markets.

3. Personal Growth and Learning: Positive relationships often expose us to different perspectives ideas and experiences. They challenge our assumptions broaden our horizons and contribute

to personal growth and learning.

Example: If you have a mentor or a close friend who has a different background or expertise nurturing that relationship can provide valuable insights and expand your knowledge and understanding of various subjects or industries.

In conclusion networking developing effective interpersonal skills and nurturing positive relationships are integral to personal and professional success. These practices enhance opportunities create supportive environments and contribute to personal growth and fulfillment.

# 8

# Taking Action and Persisting Towards Success

Dreams alone are but fleeting sparks; it is action and persistence that fan them into the blazing fires of success. In this chapter, we embark on a dynamic expedition into the realms of determination and unwavering commitment. We'll confront the nemesis of procrastination and the shadows of fear of failure, learning how to wrest control from their grip. An action-oriented approach will become your beacon as we navigate the path to making things happen, converting dreams into reality. The enduring qualities of persistence and resilience will be your armor, shielding you from the storms of adversity. This chapter serves as your arsenal of motivation and resolve, providing you with the strategies and mindset to overcome obstacles on your journey to success. As we delve into the essence of taking action and persisting, we set the stage for a transformative odyssey where your unwavering determination is the compass guiding you toward your goals.

8.1 Overcoming Procrastination and Fear of Failure:

Procrastination and fear of failure are common obstacles to success. Overcoming these challenges is crucial for achieving one's goals. Procrastination is the act of delaying or putting off tasks often due to a lack of motivation or fear of failure. Fear of failure on the other hand is the apprehension or anxiety about not meeting expectations or experiencing negative consequences.

To overcome procrastination it is important to understand the underlying reasons for it. One strategy is to break tasks into smaller manageable chunks. By focusing on completing smaller portions the overall task feels less overwhelming making it easier to get started. Setting specific deadlines and creating a schedule can also help combat procrastination.

Moreover addressing the fear of failure requires a shift in mindset. Embracing failure as a learning opportunity can help alleviate anxiety. Recognize that failure is a natural part of the growth process and an opportunity for personal development. By reframing failure as a stepping stone to success one can overcome the fear associated with it allowing for greater progress and achievement.

For example imagine someone who wants to start a small business but keeps putting it off due to fear of failure. By breaking down the tasks into smaller steps such as conducting market research creating a business plan and seeking funding the person can gradually overcome the procrastination barrier. By re-framing failure as an opportunity to learn and grow they can take the necessary risks and pursue their entrepreneurial goals.

8.2 Adopting an Action-Oriented Approach: Making Things Happen:

An action-oriented approach is essential for achieving success. Simply having a vision or goal is not enough; taking consistent action is key. An action-oriented mindset involves actively seeking opportunities setting clear objectives and implementing strategies to achieve those objectives.

By being proactive and taking initiative individuals can create their own success. Instead of waiting for opportunities to present themselves they actively seek them out. This could involve networking reaching out to potential mentors or taking on new challenges.

Additionally setting clear objectives ensures that efforts are directed towards specific outcomes. SMART (Specific Measurable Achievable Relevant Time-bound) goals are particularly effective in this regard. Breaking down goals into smaller milestones helps track progress and provides motivation along the way.

For example let's consider someone who aspires to become a professional writer. Instead of waiting for a publishing company to approach them they can take an action-oriented approach by actively submitting their work to publishers and literary agents. They can set a goal to write a certain number of pages or chapters each day and seek feedback from professionals in the industry. By consistently taking action and pursuing opportunities they increase their chances of achieving their writing aspirations.

8.3 The Power of Persistence and Resilience in Achieving Success:

Persistence and resilience are crucial qualities for achieving success. Persistence involves continuing one's efforts in the face of obstacles and setbacks while resilience refers to the ability to bounce back and recover from challenges or failures.

Success rarely comes easily and setbacks are inevitable. However those who are persistent and resilient are more likely to overcome obstacles and reach their goals. They view challenges as learning experiences and opportunities for growth enabling them to persist despite difficulties.

By staying committed to their goals and maintaining a positive mindset individuals can push through challenging times. They adapt their strategies and seek alternative paths when faced with setbacks. They learn from their mistakes and use them as stepping stones to future success.

An excellent example of persistence and resilience can be seen in the story of Thomas Edison. Despite facing numerous failures while inventing the light bulb Edison remained persistent and resilient. He once said "I have not failed. I've just found 10000 ways that won't work." His unwavering determination eventually led to success and revolutionized the world.

In conclusion overcoming procrastination and fear of failure adopting an action-oriented approach and embodying persistence and resilience are essential for achieving success. By addressing these challenges and embracing these qualities individuals can make tangible progress towards their goals and live a more fulfilling and successful life.

# 9

# Maintaining Work-Life Balance

In the hustle and bustle of life's demands, it's easy to lose sight of the delicate equilibrium between work and the richness of personal living. In this chapter, we embark on a vital exploration into the art of balancing the scales, ensuring that the demands of work don't overshadow the essence of life itself. We'll recognize the significance of personal well-being, understanding that it is the foundation upon which all successes are built. Strategies for managing stress and avoiding the harrowing abyss of burnout will be unveiled as your lifelines. Harmonious relationships, both at home and in your career, will be your compass in navigating the seas of fulfillment. This chapter serves as your sanctuary for restoring balance, providing you with the insights and techniques to harmonize your life. As we delve into the essence of maintaining work-life balance, we set the stage for a life where you flourish not only in your career but also in the joys, passions, and relationships that make life truly meaningful.

9.1 Recognizing and Prioritizing Personal Well-being:

Recognizing and prioritizing personal well-being is crucial for maintaining a healthy and balanced lifestyle. It involves paying attention to various aspects of our physical mental and emotional health. By recognizing the signs and symptoms of stress or burnout we can take proactive measures to address them.

For example let's say you notice that you have been feeling exhausted irritable and experiencing difficulty concentrating. These could be signs of mental and emotional fatigue. Recognizing these signs allows you to prioritize your well-being by taking breaks engaging in self-care activities like exercise or hobbies and seeking support from friends family or professionals if needed.

Another example is recognizing the importance of physical well-being. This involves taking care of your body through regular exercise eating a balanced diet getting enough sleep and attending to any medical concerns. By prioritizing physical well-being you can improve your overall health energy levels and resilience to stress.

9.2 Strategies for Managing Stress and Avoiding Burnout:

Managing stress and avoiding burnout is essential for maintaining a healthy and productive life. Here are some strategies to help with this:

1. Time management: Prioritize tasks and create a schedule that allows for breaks and relaxation. Avoid overcommitting yourself and learn to say no when necessary.

2. Stress reduction techniques: Practice relaxation techniques like deep breathing meditation or yoga. Engaging in activities you enjoy such as listening to music spending time in nature or pursuing hobbies can also help reduce stress.

3. Setting boundaries: Learn to set healthy boundaries in your personal and professional life. Communicate your needs and limits to others and don't take on more responsibilities than you can handle.

4. Self-care: Engage in self-care activities that promote well-being such as exercising regularly getting enough sleep eating nutritious meals and taking time for hobbies and relaxation.

5. Seek support: Build a support network with friends family or colleagues who can provide a listening ear or offer assistance when needed. Consider seeking professional help from therapists or counselors if stress levels become overwhelming.

9.3 Creating Harmonious Relationships and Finding Fulfillment in Life:

Creating harmonious relationships and finding fulfillment in life is essential for overall well-being and happiness. Here are a few examples of how to cultivate positive relationships and find fulfillment:

1. Communication and empathy: Cultivate open and honest communication with others practicing active listening and empathy. This helps create deeper connections and understanding in relationships.

2. Building supportive networks: Surround yourself with positive and supportive people who inspire and uplift you. Foster relationships that bring out the best in you and provide a sense of belonging.

3. Nurturing personal growth: Engage in activities that promote personal growth and self-improvement. This could involve pursuing educational opportunities setting personal goals or exploring new hobbies and interests.

4. Finding purpose and meaning: Reflect on what brings you joy and fulfillment in life. Identify your values passions and interests and find ways to align your daily activities with them. This can provide a sense of purpose and fulfillment.

5. Practicing gratitude: Cultivate a mindset of gratitude by acknowledging and appreciating the positive aspects of your life. This can enhance overall well-being and satisfaction.

In summary recognizing and prioritizing personal well-being managing stress maintaining harmonious relationships and finding fulfillment can greatly contribute to living a balanced and fulfilling life. These strategies require self-awareness intentionality and consistent effort but the rewards are worth it in terms of improved mental emotional and physical well-being.

# 10

# Celebrating Success and Embracing Growth

Success is not a solitary event but a continuous journey, and the milestones along the way are worth celebrating as we forge ahead. In this chapter, we embark on a joyful exploration of recognizing achievements and nurturing growth. We'll acknowledge the importance of celebrating milestones, both big and small, as a source of motivation and gratification. Embracing continuous learning will be the heart of our journey, for growth knows no bounds. Here, you'll discover the beauty of expanding horizons, setting new goals, and pursuing fresh opportunities. This chapter serves as your inspiration and affirmation, providing you with the insights and encouragement to keep reaching for the stars. As we delve into the essence of celebrating success and embracing growth, we set the stage for a life where each achievement is a stepping stone to an even brighter tomorrow, a life where the pursuit of excellence is a never-ending adventure.

10.1 Acknowledging and Celebrating Milestones and Achievements:

Acknowledging and celebrating milestones and achievements is important as it helps us recognize and appreciate our progress boosts motivation and instills a sense of accomplishment. This can be done individually or in a team setting.

Example 1: Imagine you have been working on a project for several months. After successfully completing it you organize a team meeting to acknowledge everyone's hard work and dedication. You share the project's positive outcomes highlight the key milestones achieved and celebrate the team's achievements with some treats or a small celebration.

Example 2: In a personal context suppose you set a target to save a certain amount of money within a year. When you reach that milestone you may choose to acknowledge it by treating yourself to something special going out for dinner at your favorite restaurant or even taking a short trip to celebrate your financial achievement.

10.2 Embracing Continuous Learning and Personal Growth:

Embracing continuous learning and personal growth involves being open to acquiring new knowledge developing skills and seeking opportunities to improve oneself. It may include attending workshops enrolling in courses reading books or seeking mentorship.

Example 1: Let's say you work in the field of digital marketing and you want to enhance your knowledge of search engine optimization (SEO). You enroll in an online course or attend a workshop specifically tailored to SEO techniques. By actively participating and learning from experts in the field you expand your skill set and stay up-to-date with the latest trends.

Example 2: In a personal growth context you may decide to learn a new musical instrument. You invest time in practicing regularly watching online tutorials and seeking guidance from a music teacher. As you progress and acquire new skills you not only experience personal growth but also gain a sense of fulfillment and satisfaction.

10.3 Expanding Your Horizons: Setting New Goals and Pursuing New Opportunities:

Expanding your horizons involves stepping out of your comfort zone setting new goals and seeking out new opportunities for personal and professional development. This helps you keep evolving discovering your potential and finding new paths to success.

Example 1: Let's say you've been working in a particular job for several years and have gained expertise in a specific area. To expand your horizons you decide to take on a new role or responsibility within your organization that challenges you in different ways. This not only helps you grow professionally but also broadens your skill set and opens doors for future career opportunities.

Example 2: On a personal level you may have always wanted to learn a foreign language and immerse yourself in a different culture. You choose to pursue this goal by enrolling in language classes joining cultural exchange programs or even planning a trip to a country where the language is spoken. By doing so you expand your horizons gain a new perspective and create opportunities for personal growth and enrichment.

In summary acknowledging and celebrating milestones and achievements embracing continuous learning and personal growth and expanding your horizons through new goals and opportunities are vital for personal and professional development. These practices contribute to a fulfilling and successful life journey.

# 11

# 100 Tips for Success

1. Set clear and achievable goals.
2. Develop a positive mindset and stay motivated.
3. Believe in yourself and your abilities.
4. Take responsibility for your actions and choices.
5. Maintain a healthy work-life balance.
6. Surround yourself with positive and supportive people.
7. Continuously learn and improve your skills.
8. Stay focused and avoid distractions.
9. Embrace failure as an opportunity to learn and grow.
10. Practice self-discipline and time management.
11. Stay adaptable and open to new ideas.
12. Take risks and step out of your comfort zone.
13. Network and build meaningful relationships.
14. Embrace challenges and see them as opportunities.
15. Prioritize your tasks and work efficiently.
16. Stay organized and maintain a clean workspace.
17. Seek feedback and use it to improve.
18. Cultivate good habits that support your goals.
19. Take care of your physical and mental health.

20. Develop strong communication skills.
21. Learn from successful people and role models.
22. Stay persistent and don't give up easily.
23. Manage stress and practice relaxation techniques.
24. Seek opportunities for personal growth and development.
25. Develop a positive attitude towards failure.
26. Stay humble and open-minded.
27. Take initiative and be proactive.
28. Set realistic deadlines and meet them.
29. Cultivate a growth mindset and embrace learning.
30. Practice gratitude and focus on the positives.
31. Develop excellent problem-solving skills.
32. Be accountable for your actions and choices.
33. Build resilience and bounce back from setbacks.
34. Stay focused on your long-term vision.
35. Practice effective decision-making.
36. Stay up to date with industry trends and developments.
37. Embrace constructive criticism and use it to improve.
38. Maintain a strong work ethic and show dedication.
39. Seek out mentors or coaches for guidance.
40. Develop excellent communication and listening skills.
41. Embrace continuous learning and improvement.
42. Practice resilience in the face of adversity.
43. Take care of your physical and mental well-being.
44. Set aside time for self-reflection and introspection.
45. Stay organized and manage your time effectively.
46. Develop a strong sense of self-belief and confidence.
47. Celebrate your achievements no matter how small.
48. Stay adaptable and embrace change.
49. Learn from your mistakes and use them as stepping stones.

50. Prioritize your tasks and focus on what's important.

51. Develop a strong work ethic and show dedication to your goals.

52. Stay curious and never stop learning.

53. Find your passion and pursue it relentlessly.

54. Surround yourself with positive and like-minded people.

55. Take care of your physical health by exercising regularly.

56. Develop strong problem-solving and critical thinking skills.

57. Take calculated risks and embrace uncertainty.

58. Continually challenge yourself and seek personal growth.

59. Learn effective communication skills to build strong relationships.

60. Stay focused on your long-term goals but be adaptable in your approach.

61. Develop resilience to bounce back from setbacks.

62. Learn from successful individuals in your field.

63. Develop a strong work ethic and consistently put in the effort.

64. Embrace failure as a learning opportunity and don't be afraid to make mistakes.

65. Take care of your mental well-being by practicing self-care and mindfulness.

66. Set clear priorities and manage your time effectively.

67. Surround yourself with positive influences and supportive people.

68. Continuously educate yourself and stay updated with industry trends.

69. Stay persistent and persevere through challenges.

70. Take calculated risks and step out of your comfort zone.

71. Celebrate both small and big accomplishments along the

way.

72. Cultivate strong problem-solving and decision-making skills.

73. Foster a growth mindset and embrace continuous learning.

74. Maintain a healthy work-life balance to avoid burnout.

75. Seek feedback and actively work on improving yourself.

76. Develop effective communication skills to connect with others.

77. Stay adaptable and open-minded to embrace change.

78. Practice gratitude and appreciate the journey towards success.

79. Take responsibility for your actions and hold yourself accountable.

80. Network and build relationships with influential people in your field.

81. Keep your goals in focus and regularly evaluate your progress.

82. Stay disciplined and organized in your daily routines.

83. Keep your mindset positive and overcome self-doubt.

84. Develop empathy and understand the perspectives of others.

85. Practice active listening to build strong relationships.

86. Learn from unsuccessful attempts and use them as stepping stones.

87. Continually challenge yourself to go beyond your comfort zone.

88. Stay committed to your long-term vision even in the face of obstacles.

89. Take care of your physical and mental well-being through self-care practices.

90. Set clear boundaries to prioritize your time and energy

effectively.

91. Seek out mentors or role models who can guide and inspire you.

92. Learn to manage stress and practice relaxation techniques.

93. Continuously update your skills and stay relevant in your industry.

94. Be adaptable and embrace change as an opportunity for growth.

95. Foster a positive work environment by supporting and encouraging your colleagues.

96. Take regular breaks to recharge and refocus your energy.

97. Stay true to your values and maintain your integrity.

98. Celebrate the successes of others and build a strong support network.

99. Reflect on your progress and make adjustments along the way.

100. Remember that success is a journey not a destination. Enjoy the process and learn from every experience.

www.ingramcontent.com/pod-product-compliance
Lightning Source LLC
LaVergne TN
LVHW010437070526
838199LV00066B/6053